Riceland

by CL Bledsoe

Englewood, NJ

ISBN 978-1-936373-37-6
Published in the United States by Unbound Content, LLC,
Englewood, NJ.
Cover art: Leaning Barn ©2012 Jillian Meyer
Author photo: ©2013 Jillian Meyer

Riceland
First edition 2013

For Wilma and Billy, and Julie and Mike

Table of Contents

Here I can only say that in the people of this country you care most for, pretty nearly without exception you must reckon in traits, needs, diseases, and above all natural habits, differing from our own, of a casualness, apathy, self-interest, unconscious, offhand, and deliberated cruelty, in relation towards extra-human life and toward negroes, terrible enough to freeze your blood or break your heart or to propel you toward murder; and that you must reckon them as "innocent" even of the worst of this; and must realize that it is at least unlikely that enough of the causes can ever be altered, or pressures withdrawn, to make much difference.

—James Agee, *Let Us Now Praise Famous Men*

Roaches

When I was a boy   I heard roaches sing.
It only happened at night   after Mom got sick
and went back to St. Louis. Dad worked long hours
and stayed drunk. Every day,
I came in from the rice fields
        too sweaty to sleep but too tired not to
        pressed my cheek to the wall beside the bed
        because it was cool
and they were in there   singing.

This was different from in the fields. I'd heard mosquitoes,
but never roaches, sing. I'd felt water moccasins
        stroke my leg like fingers as they swam past
        felt the shovel   dribble mud down my back
        like a heavy breeze   the dull gray levies
        that stretched out before me that day
        and would the next
        felt the weight of my father's tired muscles
        as we dragged him from his truck to bed
        the quiet of the house since Mom was gone;
I forgot it all, and listened to them sing.

In the mornings, I woke   staggered
        into the dusty light of my father's truck
        and tucked the memory of my nights away
        under the hard slap of the sun on my back
        and the drunken jokes of farmers
        that didn't make any sense.
I sank into the mud of those fields

and into myself   waiting

until night came
when I could crawl into bed
press my face against the wall
and listen.

Feeding the Fish

My father woke before dawn to feed the fish
      fed me   if I rose early enough and caught him
    runny eggs, coffee, under-done bacon
while he sat reading westerns at the kitchen table
    so quiet   Death would've tiptoed

The morning   washed over the dirty white curtains
    watched me stand   just behind his back
    working toward the courage
      to ask for more toast

Then into his truck   the sun so bright through the dust
    of the morning   I closed my eyes to all things
sat   in the cab   while he stacked 50 pound bags of fish feed
    back bent
      strong   like the arc
      of a sledgehammer

    Later I climbed
scared / tired / cold into the aluminum boat
      watched his hard arms move
  land
    water
      sky
all around us til it looked best
    everything blue / warming / his slit bag
dribbling food   over the side like sand   pouring
    through his rusted hands

CL Bledsoe

Fish trailed us like children
       until winter
when they lay fat
       and we dragged our nets

Riceland

Toasting Buns

The hardwood sent sharp thrills
through the soles of our feet, numbing
us with the shock of winter's burning
cold, until we learned to throw an old shirt,
blanket, anything on the floor first,
and slide it to the bathroom.

We woke early and rose slowly,
like dough under our blankets,
until we heard the dull cursing of our father
as he stepped into the winter air after showering,
then it was a race to get in next.

The damp tile welcomed us into a cloud of steam
and a promise of warm water where we could boil
off the cold. Then a dash to the closet for clothes,
and a sprint to the old butane heater to dress.

There's a trick to toasting your buns—
you have to keep your mind on them, or they'll burn.
My sister was like a microwave, cooking her front
the whole time while her back sat in a cold spot.

I was rotisserie, baking for a few seconds then turning;
as soon as one side browned I flipped it
for an even tan. Too soon, it would be time to go.
then we'd sit right on top

until we'd scorched our bottoms so badly
there was nothing for it: with a little yelp we'd hop
off and run outside with enough courage burned
into us to last to the bus stop.

Escape

Old enough to walk, but still shaky
on new legs, the little blonde girl
I used to be before Dad made Mom
cut my hair. Mom, only a few years
before the life sighed out of her, undressed
me for bath time, but left the bathroom
door slightly open. A mistake. I broke

and ran, blew through the brown carpeted hall
in a whirl and burst into the living room just
as my brother and his friend, Crow, came in,
chattering, probably about Zeppelin's last
album, Aerosmith's reformation, the final
stake in the heart of disco.

Crow greeted this naked Zephyr with a laugh,
a snide comment. I circled them three times,
squealing, arms in the air, a magic circle
to claim them, and ran back
to the bathroom and into mom's arms.

Blackberry Bushes at the Silo

Harvest time reminded our boy minds
of death. Trucks burped thunder as their loads of rice
were augured out into the concrete-lined pit;
a screw in the bottom churned the grain,
sucked it into the silos with a shuffling sound
like sand trying to whistle.
We breathed in chaff and dust,
waiting for them to go for another load.

Then, quick as thieves, we laid a rain-warped board
across the void. Some kid had fallen in years ago,
and the screw wrenched his arm right off,
crushed his legs, squashed him almost to death
because he didn't listen: our parents told us this story
with the same lips they used to kiss us goodnight.

The object was to stand in the middle of the board
while the older boys stomped on the ends.
We had to ride the plank like a log roll.
It would be hours before anyone came back
to empty their trucks, time enough to dig the bodies out.

This day, Justin, runt son of an old drunk
who hung around the farm and got in the way
of work watched me cross halfway,
watched the boys thump the plank, sending me surfing;
saw me fall to my knees and crawl back to safety,
while the older ones laughed.

They turned to Justin, all teeth and tans,
and he spooked and ran, chased by fists
and threats to lock him in with the rats
so he'd suffocate as the silo filled with grain.
We caught him, tripped-up in the corpse
of an old fence. He offered up to us a bleeding,
black-fisted handful of blackberries
from the bush beside his head,
doing its damnedest to strangle the rusted barbed-wire.

Grinning like skulls, the smaller boys snatched
the berries up, and smacked loud in time to the thud
of fists teaching poor Justin's bones.

Big Winter

Kids came from the whole neighborhood
to sled the big hill behind our house—usually

reserved for dove hunting, the occasional tumble—now

covered in a thick white. We'd cajole any adult sober
enough to drive to Hunt's Tire Service

for a tractor tire inner-tube because the old man

wouldn't sell them to kids in winter—he didn't approve
of what we'd do as soon as we got home.

The boys pushed the girls before they were ready, bullied

the younger kids, vying for the record for longest
slide. We'd trudge inside the house for hot chocolate, take

turns in front of the butane heater playing Atari 2600

while our fingers thawed, then race back to the hill,
every year, the same group of us, perfecting our techniques,

inching farther and farther down the hill, into the valley.

Once, Keith, a near-adult the girls went red around,
took a turn. We taunted him, tried to scare him with stories

of sticks popping the tube, kids flipping and sliding down

on their faces. He listened, serious, nodding, then jumped
on and slid down, across the valley below to the frozen

lake, and across most of that. A wave of girls and younger

boys plunged down to help him carry the inner-tube
back up, smiling and waving, while we all grumbled.

The Pelican

It was late fall when I first saw the white blur
drop to the surface of the stock pond,
with a low call, like a flooded boat motor.
It was too big to be anything but holy.

Dad said it was lost, said the storm
must've blown it there. "It's beautiful," I said.
"It's eating my damn fish," he said.
"And if it doesn't die, I'll kill it."

I worked out plans to stalk him, hide
in the back of his truck and jump out the moment
he raised his gun. I was his son;
he would forgive me. But all I ever did was sit
on the corner post on top of the hill above the pond
and watch its silky neck straining down
to eat our livelihood. I was his son.

Two days later, the storm came back.
Wind scraped the sides of our house
like the fingernails of witches,
and I sat in the bedroom and prayed.

The next morning, I found it lying on the bank,
its feet submerged,
a catfish hanging out of its beak.
        I could see the tips of its wings, stained black.
        I could see its white body;
        I could see its blood.

The WABAC Machine

Saturday morning is a eulogy for Memphis
wrestling, *Dick Williams' Magic Hour*, the optimism
of emphatic ignorance. The Lone Ranger wears his mask
because he is a ghost, not a coward. The Rifleman can choose
not to use his gun
                    unless someone really deserves
to be shot. Even then, he just wounds them. The smell
of horses, gunpowder burning
on the tongue. (Bad) men screaming. I would brush
my teeth with a piece of leather, go without bathing
every day, and I would not cry, even when the arrows
pierced my skin. They always grazed anyway.
                                            Bullwinkle

was my father as much as anyone whose name
I happen to share. Back then, we didn't know
we were worthless, so we did great things. Back then,
Saturday morning was Sunday comin' down. All
was forgiven in the enthusiasm of youth. The Noble
Savage may torture, but he never betrays
his nature, Kemo Sabe. The dusty plains of boyhood
stretch ever onward un-owned, interrupted only by
commercial breaks, sugared crunchy bits
to turn the milk pink.

                    Saturday morning tells us a man can paint
his face and dance for children and still look his father
in the eye. A man can play pretend well past
boyhood and still walk the aisles of Piggly Wiggly. These men.
Outside, the sun is beginning to rise and the Space Cadet
can't find his decoder ring. Soon, there will be chores: fish
to feed, fields to walk as the sun scolds him awake. Bullies

who don't seem to understand that bad guys don't win.
He will not cry. Even when disappointment comes for his heart
like a gang of outlaws. He will stand tall, face them down.
Evil clouds the aim, after all.

Envoi

The church ladies all ached
with age. Their hair stiff as steel wool,
faces grayed as frozen meat,
flashing quick smiles
when Mom served
pineapple upside down cake
on china from the hutch we mustn't touch:
oil the pan first next time, don't beat
the eggs so much, this was something they knew more
about than this young, pretty
girl who lived in her mind and hid
stacks of Harlequin Romance novels.
Born in St. Louis and stuck in a town of 7000
souls; *Wynne, The City With a Smile*
(in old English, she once told them, *wynne* meant *joy*
and tried to smile when they said *college
sure didn't teach you how to cook*).

A man once came to our door selling encyclopedias.
The church ladies warned her—
*he'll ask if your husband's here,
and when he finds out you're alone, a little
thing like you?* They ushered him away, threatened
to call the police, their husbands; *we're armed,*
they said, these women who knew as much
about the world as a catfish knows
about life outside the pond. My mother caught him
on the way out. "Ask anyone around,

I've been selling this route for years," he said.
"Those women are fools."
She saw something she'd almost forgotten
in his angry eyes
and bought everything he had.

Skinning Catfish

A mass of writhing life in the stained white basin,
each struggling to die the slowest. My father hung

one from a dull hook dangling over the basin
and whittled it down to meat in seconds. Starting

with the gray cap of skin, then fins placed where ears
should be; talking about the Crop Report, the bastards

in Washington, the lack of rain, while the customers
watched, mostly women, mostly black, mostly poorer

than us, somewhere in between Roman spectacle
and grocer. Hear tell they taught a monkey to talk

up at the University of Arkansas, but all it wanted
to talk about was the price of bananas. Even the lemon-

suckers would laugh eventually; they were there to listen
to him lie just as much as watch his knife dance through flesh.

The Pig Farmer

The old black man who came for fish guts
wouldn't step in the door of my father's fish shop.
He parked his tattered truck, faded
to the gray color Death's old clothes must be,
stood outside and waited while my father hefted
the gut tubs on his shoulder one at a time,
and handed them out.
Then the old man dumped them in the back of his truck
with a look on his face like we were living wrong.

It shamed me.
When my father passed the second tub out to him,
I followed and took a good look at the truck and the mass
of fish bones, heads, and fins. There was no tailgate;
he had to pile the guts up right behind the cab or they'd fall
out. Even then, I bet he had to drive real slow.

Inside the fish shop, there was blood. The floor was worn
a dirty lavender, broken up by yellow dots of fly poison,
except for two perfect circles of clean concrete
where the gut tubs had been.

The old man set the empty tub down. My father
handed him the third one. After he'd emptied it,
the old man threw a nod at my father
and had to crank his truck four times
before it started. I stood outside while my father

CL Bledsoe

washed blood off the floor with a hose,
letting the water drain outside in a dirty stream.
He scrubbed until the concrete shone like river mud,
and brought the tubs in, the first two at once, then the third.
Pig-smell hung in the air from the old man
like Absalom in a tree. Soon it would be supplanted by the stink
of fish. I imagined it stuck to my clothes and would linger
no matter how often they were washed.
Inside, my father sat down to read the paper.

Riceland

We sat in line,
a dozen trucks
 in front, a dozen behind,
all grey or faded
red, the colors
of dust, rust, time.
Rice chaff filled our lungs,
covered our clothes, our faces;
we could hardly tell brown
from pink. All of us swarthy,
dirty.

My brother's arm, thick
as oak, thrown
over the window
sill of the truck door, his
cap pushed back.
I reached up, lifted
my new Riceland cap
my father had given me the day
before and smoothed
my hair, as I'd seen him do,
trying to look
frustrated,
annoyed,
spiteful.

Beside us,
beyond us, the sky

stretched blue, the land
stretched green, all rice
fields, all flooded with color.
My brother fiddled
with the radio, found only
country, switched it off, tapped
his fingers twice and turned it back on.
"Old piece of shit," he said.
"Piece of crap," I said.

We pulled up,
got out. My brother went in. I stood
aside, seeing as if for the first time
the dryers towering,
concrete colored, the tallest
things in the world.

My brother came out, ash faced,
a wad in his hand he stuffed
in his pocket to get it out of sight.
"Wait all fucking day for four and a half,"
he said and pulled
up to dump the load
while I practiced
scowling.

On the ride back
to the field, we topped out

Riceland

at a rumbling forty, listened to more
country music,
watched the land slide
by like clouds. I was learning
to complain, learning
impatience with the enthusiasm
of a dog chasing a stick.
My uncle in the combine
met us and we waited
while the radio twanged.
"Come on now," I said, pleased
to be the first to complain.
My brother scowled
and said nothing.

Bush-hogging

Most times he waited till the grass
had grown nearly to the cows' asses,

before he climbed into the tattered seat
of that old tractor, red as a beet

left in the sun, the same color his knees
would be from an afternoon of being slapped by weeds.

He'd run over trash, neighbors, or anything slow
when he'd finally made up his mind to mow,

He'd see me watching and raise a toughened hand
then sail out over the newly revealed land.

Mike's Room

Two months wasted at college brought my brother
back to work long hours in the Fish Shack, filleting,
dicing, however you please. He covered the wood

paneling of the converted garage with posters
of the Guess Who and Mountain, shelves lined
with boxes of 8-tracks, stacks of albums, piles
of cassettes threatening to topple. A wonderland

of baseball cards and 70s comic books. Evenings he
laid in his giant bed, listening to:
        The Who: *Live at Leeds*
        Cream: *Live Volume 2*
        Jethro Tull: *Original Masters*
and dreamed of being a drummer, touring
Monterey, the Isle of Wight.

He took any excuse for a road trip, and in the car,
he quizzed me on FM music until
I learned Page from Blackmore, Kay from Burdon.
"Listen," he'd say, shushing me for a solo

and then dissecting it afterwards. He devoured
Destroyer serials, quoted Mark Twain and Mel
Brooks, action movies and Shakespeare. "Remember"
he'd say: "No matter where you go, there you are."

CL Bledsoe

The Old Ways

When I got home from school,
the calf was already hanging
by its tendons from an old single-tree hitch.
My father held a Budweiser in one hand,
a butcher knife in the other.
He tossed my backpack to the side,
like things were about to happen.

I tried to nod on cue as he explained
the hanging job, the right way to cut the meat.
He talked about the good old days when he was a boy,
how they made shoes out of the hide
and wasted nothing.

And I watched, brother; I drank in every drop
of blood, sweat, and BS he threw out.
I painted my father's sure hands
somewhere permanent inside me—
the way his knife slid through the calf's flesh
like it was smoke.

And when he passed the blade to me,
I did my best not to chew the meat up too badly.
He nodded, acting satisfied
as I worried the hide off the thing,
glancing at him to call me off
before I made a mess of it.

After a while he stepped up and slid its coat off.
I fell back, sweaty.

Riceland

Then I ran to get the water hose
and cleared the blood off the grass
after he'd finished. I tried to stand
in the same top-heavy lean as my father
and admire an afternoon's work,
like a man would.

He walked over to the cooler.
got out a Budweiser and handed it to me,
like I was finally his son.
I pulled the tab and metal tongue out
and drank it down.

When we went inside—
my father shining like a knife blade—
I went into the bathroom, locked the door
and puked it all out.

Afternoon Walk

I found them in the shade
of an old pecan tree. The cow moaned

on its belly, tried to lift
its weight on one leg, but slipped

in the mud, the leaves,
and its own blood which stained

the valley floor. My father, alone, red-
skinned as that blood, too focused to even

cuss anymore, murmured
soothing words as he struggled

to secure a harness impossibly
around the shoulders of the dead calf still

halfway inside its mother. An old
rust-colored tractor idled on the other end

of the harness. He pulled, one foot
on the cow's rump, the calf

still, my father frantic
until he saw me. "Tractor!"

he yelled. I moved, never mind the fear,
the blood, never mind that I couldn't drive the thing.

Riceland

He barked orders, steered me as though I were
an engine, my arms, the gear-shift,

my feet, the peddles. I eased
forward, watched him pull

as I kept the wheel straight. The calf
shifted; the cow lowered its head

as though concentrating on a difficult thought. The calf's
corpse squeezed out and landed

on my father, who fell to the ground, dragged
by the harness, which jerked forward

as the tractor lurched
into the tree and stalled out.

Ripen

The thin fiberglass of the tractor's cab gave little shade.
We moved too slow for a breeze, raising levees
in curves that made no sense to me.
Straight, young spears of rice, green and thick as hair
covered the field's bone-white dust. Soon, we'd flood it
and spend our days patching breaks,
throwing mud into rushing water
as my father had done for twice my lifetime.

There was an old house on the far side, its walls drooped,
with holes worn in its roof where birds got in.
We pulled into the overgrown driveway
and parked under a dead oak to eat lunch.
I pointed at a spot of green. "Watermelon," Dad said,
"Not ripe yet, though. Too small."
We sat on the tailgate, swallowing white bread, lunchmeat,
water. I kept glancing back at the vine.

"Someone must've spit seeds over there," he said.
"We should come back," I said. "When it's grown."
"The water will kill it," he said, wiping his hands
on his pants. On the tractor,
I watched the lines grow over the field,
the house getting closer.
My father ignored the heat, the dust, mosquitoes,
his red skin already ruined from years of sun,
while I burned behind him
wishing time would stop, speed up, something.

The Cry of the Catfish

I know how to grow things, and I know how to kill them.
My father taught me; he made his living killing things.
            He raised them for it.

Fish were the first he taught me. Even sober,
my father could skin a catfish faster than it could die.
Their little mouths worked,
but they didn't make a sound,
as he'd snatch one out of the dirty white basin,
hang it like a thief on a cross,
and cut it. He did it so fast,
by the time you wanted to look away,
they were already skinned,
diced, or filleted, cut up however you pleased.

Hunting squirrels was next. He could
hear one slap a nut against a branch
a mile away. There was a science to
the way he'd hand me his beer with a low sigh
            raise his .22
            and pick one off
when I couldn't even tell what tree it was in.

They barked at us sometimes;
he'd let one live long enough for that,
and I'd get a shot at it. As he skinned them,
I'd watch his gnarled, oaken hands
pull the fur over their heads
like he was undressing them for bed.

He taught me how to raise chickens and cows,
and he taught me deer.
He taught me quiet, the first rule of hunting.
And so neither he nor I made a sound
the day I headed off to raise a life of my own,
sit back and watch it grow feather and fat,
and take my knife to it.

Huntington's Disease

1 Brushy Lake

The ancient pecan tree ached for sky, throwing
nuts like hail stones onto the dirt road bordering
the milo field. Mom spread a blanket across
the still-green brass beneath the limbs stretched

like sea anemones. From the green and wheat-colored
basket, she drew fried chicken, mashed potatoes,
biscuits with homemade jam, corn from the garden
by Mamaw's house, celery sticks stuffed

with pimento cheese, chicken livers to split
with Julie Beth. They waited and watched Dad
roll up the road from checking the pump
at Brushy Lake, or cross from the rice field

on the back side, idling along in the old '57 Ford,
not even raising a cloud on the dusty road. He'd
ease up with his door already open because
he never closed it, slide out, and run water

over his dusty hands from the cooler in the back.
Mom and Julie would run up, hand him iced tea
and lead him back to the blanket, shaded
from the massive blue of Arkansas sky, a stain

of white for clouds, while cattle chewed grass tips
on the other side of the fence. On the way home,
Dad took Julie, following Mom who tapped
her brakes at each curve as though she feared

losing control at any moment. He cursed
her caution instead of wondering what caused it,
and rode her bumper home, the second in a line
stretching down the highway.

2 Thanksgiving

My father's nine surviving siblings gathered
each year in the house on the hill for Thanksgiving

dinner. The Aunts lined all the food up
on Aunt Louise's counters, desserts on the kitchen

table. Mom would bring pineapple slices with a dollop
of mayo and a slice of American cheese on top,

jello from a box which was promptly placed
in the back under the cabinets. How to compete

with a family of Southern epicurists who guarded
their brother nearly as jealously as their recipes

for ooey-gooey cake, Mississippi mud pie, sweet
cornbread, uncured ham, turkey so tender it falls

from the bone, green bean casserole ... Julie Beth,
who loved pineapple, helped finish the plate off. Mike,

who loved jello, handled that. "There's a lot of food,"
Dad would say, "Next year, you should bring less."

3 Avon

A quick ride down the hill to cousin
Shirley's to pick up Avon, Julie Beth

looking forward to playing with her second
cousins, Mary Beth and Lisa, when suddenly

Mom's legs stop working. Not asleep, not
cramping just not responding. Panic and then

the emergency brake, Julie Beth surprised and Mom
scared as she began to recognize patterns

from her father's failing years. A moment to collect
and Mom took the long loop back up the hill

slowly; Julie Beth watched her cousins' house falling
out of sight afraid to complain because Mom was still
    crying.

4 Johnny Hill

Summers when Mom was off from teaching
we vacationed on a family friend's horse farm,
slept in the bunk house, fished in his lake.

Julie taught me to drive on the long gravel road
between the gate and the dock, me sitting
on her lap while she worked the pedals. Mom

wore such fancy clothes for a vacation, we thought,
vivd green vests and feathery hats, while we wore jeans,
tee-shirts. She, afraid to stray too far from the building, sat

in a folding chair, prim and straight, frowned
as her legs twitched, her hands fidgeted like wayward
children, while we snuck off to stick flowers in the liquid

hydrogen tank and stomp them to see them shatter.
There was something draining in the air other
than mosquitoes. Guests came in waves. Dad, after a few,

would dance with the ladies while Mom watched, face
twitching like her hands. But in the morning, they always
lingered in bed, Dad, dozing, Mom, finally still.

5 Bus Stop

Every school day, the nurse would help Mom walk down
the winding hill to the bus stop to meet me.

Riceland

Maybe I was twelve, maybe ten—too old
to still have Mommy meet me at the bus, especially

when, after I crossed Killough to Dodd Hill, she
would grab me in a tight hug, eyes wide

and scared like a wounded animal. I learned to dart
behind the bus, back to a side street,

and down the long line of pines to the Fish Shack
where Mike and Dad worked. The whole time,

the nurse yelled after me, "Boy, come to
your Momma!" while the other kids snickered
          and Mom said nothing.

6 *The Hill*

After school, I'd trudge the mile
through the thinning houses of the nearest
neighborhood, climb the barbed-wire fence twined

with rust-colored cow hair that marked
our land, and cross the sea of weeds and yellow
bitter-weed flowers by the stock pond, to the big hill

behind our house where, most days, I could already hear
Mom at the back door, moaning out over the hills
like a wraith. This was what it was to be trapped

CL Bledsoe

in a body she could barely control, a mind crumbling
apart. Dad spent long nights out drinking, Mike and Julie
disappeared when they could. Mom would moan

until she heard Dad stumble home, then collapse
into a hoarse sleep. I thought she was trying to break
my mind. Each night, I dreamed the secret of escape: all I had

to do was push my legs beyond the limits of endurance
to run faster than a fox who's caught the scent
of rabbit, faster than the rabbit who escapes; as long

as no human eyes saw me, I could be free. Mornings, I woke
in a stiff body, spent awkward days avoiding the eyes
of classmates, teachers with underpaid consciences.
Afternoons,

I stood, with the wild wheat swaying in the breeze,
and pounded my thighs to force them to run, to run, to run.

Dear Cow,

I'm sorry I shot you with my second-hand
rifle when I was twelve. I hated you
because you were my father's, and he'd cussed me
the night before. The rifle, I hated the same.
He only gave it to me because he thought
I was a nancy-boy and didn't know how to kill. I thought
he was right. My father said cows
have thick hides, and you were so far away.
I heard you moaning before they found you, bleeding out.
It hurt me. Not as much as I hurt you, I know.

CL Bledsoe

Broken-Bottomed Chairs

1

The straight iron legs of the kitchen
chair dig into the linoleum, leaving light
gashes from the table to the fridge. I stand
on its unmoored black cushion to reach
into the freezer. Plastic
whiskey bottles with their spouts
cut off, filled with frozen lard rest to one side.
Their mottled white fat begs use; it leaks a loam smell.
I stick my nose in, breathe deeply, imagining bacon ice cream.

2

I will lie and say I was ten, twelve, old enough
to be unattended, but then why did I need
the chair to stand on in front of the old stove
with burners so coated in grease splatter
we let them burn clean before each use?
Pancakes were easiest, ham steak, another
chair for the oven whose filament caught
fire sometimes, giving biscuits a smoky, charbroiled edge.

3

Wild children, my sister and I nested like rats,
rearranging furniture to fit our games—Crocodiles
in the Carpet (don't get bitten!) or Table Slide!

My favorite was when we'd pull a chair
up to a closet and hide in the plywood
cubby-hole up top. Even above the piano, we pasted
pictures cut from Mom's magazines, scribbled
our names in crayon, left notes for each other: "Meet
me in Mom's closet. Urgent! Signed Boo." I'd run
to Mom's bedroom, climb a kitchen chair
to find my sister, whispering so the Calvary
wouldn't come for our collection of scalps,
as Mom, lost, stared glazed-eyed at a point
just above and beyond the TV screen.

4

When we'd exhausted the closet clubhouse, we'd pull
a chair up to the door between the kitchen and living room,
take turns climbing up to perch, one foot on each knob
on either side and ride the door while the other
pushed. Call it sound construction; by the time
we'd outgrown this, the door was only warped so much
that it couldn't pull-to completely.

5

Mom's china cabinet stood slightly removed
from one wall. The dining room chairs huddled
around a table the polished mahogany
of a coffin, their thin frames curved

like the graceful legs of an insect. Their seats
had collapsed in on themselves, so only one or two
could be balanced upon successfully. After Mom
became sick, Dad never threw anything away.
We thought he was cheap. The house
filled with junk: Mom's old
clothes, piles of letters and magazines.

The day after Thanksgiving, three years later,
the house burned. Secretly, we were relieved
to not have to face an un-cleanable storehouse
of broken memories, until my brother and his wife threw
out the couch we had jumped on until the springs
broke, the table we used to slide down, the piano
we hid messages in, and all the old chairs
no one could've sat in even if they hadn't
burned. All of it smoke-stained and mildewed, yes,
but also ours. She spent weeks replacing everything
with new, clean, orderly furniture, chairs
you could sit on without fear of falling through
the seat, closets free of scribbles and bowed
shelves, no more clutter, no more spiders or mice
or Calvary Marauders: a house we no longer recognized.

But My Legs Remember That Road

After Huntington's Disease settled in
like an uninvited guest, my mother started
her walks. Back and forth, down the gravel road
from our house to the cattle gap, from the gap
to my aunt's house, from my aunt's, back.
It wasn't so much that she was trying to outpace
the disease; she was trying to remember
the way home, grinding each step into the gravel,
working it into her legs until they could remember for her.

I was young when this all started. I knew only
that her father died with his fist print
still buried in the metal of a car door,
so deep and perfect you could see the outline
of his wedding ring,
though he could not recall his wife's name.

She wrote, as well. Every evening, after dinner,
she copied one line after another on college-ruled paper:
her name, her birth-date, her children's names, her husband's;
things she needed to remember. We kept
these pages in her old hope chest
with her wedding gown, her photos.
But my legs also learned that road, tagging
behind her like a stray calf, the dust
that tasted like unsweetened chocolate,
the jerk of her stops and starts, the chorea
of her path, crisscrossing the gravel like a dance floor
as she fought her way back to control.

Bachelor Club

1

Dad would come in from the fields
with hungry kids to feed, set me to peeling
potatoes for German Fries, a kind of thick
hash-brown, learned from the army
like most of his dishes; get a pot
of beans going with ham hock
and pepper to taste, his true masterpiece;
served with pork steaks pasted in flour
and dunked in lard to splatter the stove
a full three minutes before he flopped them, bleeding,
on a plate. Chicken was the same, steak barely
warm when served. Once, my sister bought
butter flavored Crisco and he spread it on his
toast, thinking it was margarine, too thin
to be grease. There is a story
that Mom swatted a fly on a burger and he ate it
anyway, saying, "More protein."

2

There were aunts to take us to church and uncles
to teach us to curse. During roundups, they'd chase
me and my cousins with cattle prods, hook each other's
truck seats to their ignition coils so they'd be shocked
each time they cranked the engine. One was hit
by a train and they sent him a new pair

of boxers in the hospital. They took out ads
in the paper selling each other's possessions. Mom
used to wash our mouths out with soap if we said
"dang." Once, Julie asked the meaning
of the other name for a cat, and Mom knocked her across
the bed. Our uncles routinely called us names
we wouldn't understand the meaning of for years:
Whistle-britches, Goin' Jessie, others Mom
would've fainted dead at the sound of.
How to make her understand: it was a sign
of affection when these men took a break from playing
grab-ass in the gravel lot and dressed us down.
Theirs was not a world in which scrapes
were kissed, forks were placed properly or even
used; theirs was a world in which the soft veal
of youth is eaten, the playful is stewed.

CL Bledsoe

Hogging

We dribbled feed along the perimeter
of Brushy Lake over the side of the faded

and oft-patched aluminum boat, pulled it
up on shore and flipped it, then we walked

the levee that cut the pond from the marsh,
quiet as the Arkansas sun. The far shore

was all stumps and gumbo. Dad explained
that the momma flatheads sit on their nests

after they lay eggs, and that's when you catch
them. *You can smell meat eaters; it's an acrid,*

bitter fume in the water. They don't have teeth,
but they have barbs, which don't hurt too bad.

He pointed at a deer we'd flushed; his sleeve
rode up to reveal the ring of scars that darkened

his red skin. I stayed on the shore as he waded out
to investigate an old stump then back cause it only

held a snapping turtle. All of a sudden, he ducked
down below the surface. I was alone with the music

of frogs and cicadas until he emerged, yanking
his arm engulfed in fish flesh. He beat the thing

against the earth four or five times, but it wouldn't
let go. I pulled him onto the levee, grabbed

the fighting thing, trying to avoid its burrs. Finally,
the ancient fish let go and Dad slid his bloody arm

out. It was somewhere between silver mountain
and catfish, its sloped head whiskered like

an old man. He grabbed it by its gills and hefted
it back to the truck. Through the sliding glass

I watched it flop its massive tail as it breathed its last
out. We stopped at an Argentinian family's home—

field hands he knew, and he explained the best ways
to cook the meat. The kids took turns trying to lift it,

though it was nearly as big as them. The parents
bandaged his arm and thanked us, all smiles and shaking

heads, and we headed to check the rice fields.

Big Tom

Big Tom always wanted to piss in the catfish
vats. "How would you like it," I said, "if you
had to eat piss?" He was three or four years

my junior and listened to me ever since his father's
heart gave out and left the boy in a trailer full
of hens. One time, he decided to climb inside

the drainage pipe waiting to be put in the ground
under the road above his house and have me push
him all the way down the steep pasture hill.

He wouldn't come out afterwards because he'd covered
himself with vomit and couldn't stop crying while I
laughed and asked, "Why did you do that?" We'd take

turns running over fresh cow piles with his Dad's old
lawnmower, splattering offal in perfect rays across
the grass, trying to hit each other's legs. This was before

he started stealing, married his half-sister, abandoned
his child, and started cooking meth; back when he was
just slow and petulant cousin Tom, who Dad kept

chasing off from the farm. I caught him once, emptying
himself into a dry vat. Dad and them scrubbed them
when fish season started up, so there wasn't much harm,

and by the time I came around the corner, he was already
flowing. I watched him lift the stream up to his mouth,
pause then again. He saw the look on my face, shrugged,

and said, "It ain't the worst thing."

The Boy Across the Street From Mamaw's House

Mamaw was dying at home, which is better
than with strangers, Dad said. Across
the street, neighborhood kids lined up
to take turns on a trampoline. A girl saw me
leaving Mamaw's house, asked me to come
and play, and the boy said no, but after another
day of me not even glancing across it was him, yelling.

When I crossed the brown gravel,
he told me to stand off to the side
and watch them, so I left. The next
few days, every time I entered or left
Mamaw's house, the boy jeered
and laughed: "We're having so much fun!
You wish you were over here." Inside,
Mamaw wheezed, shrinking each time
I saw her, the white of her gown shocking-
ly vibrant against the grey room.

A couple weeks after she died, I went back
to the house on an errand for Dad. The trampoline
was empty, the boy, gone. The neighbor girl
came out and told me he'd thrown a tantrum, chased
everyone off. She'd knocked on his door
a couple times, but all he did was sit inside
and play Atari games. "He does this all the time,"
she said, "everyone will be back out

in a couple days. You should come by."
"Maybe, " I lied and walked back down
the gravel road, past the house, the muddied
yard now wonderfully and terribly quiet.

Field Fire

The wind turned
after we set the field ablaze.

My father, my brother, and I made an arc
around the diesel tank with nothing but shovels

to beat the flames. The heat
washed over us; the smell of burnt

husks and dirt filled our eyes
and everything. There was water

in a slough behind us, not enough
to jump into. There was a well

on the other side of the field. The flames
swayed toward us, hungry.

My father shoveled blackening dirt,
my brother stood and cussed, I

stood between them, trying to decide
who to follow, which to choose.

First Seizure

I woke in my brother's arms, nearly
naked, rigid as dead wood,
unable to move, speak, understand.
He threw me in the back seat, steadily
yelling at dad. "You happy now, you drunk
son of a bitch? This is what you wanted?"

My father, too worried to fight, remained silent,
even though he'd been the one to find me
in the dark quiet of night, shuddering, my mouth
filling with vomit. Still half-drunk from the night
before, he'd grabbed a towel, saved me
from choking in my sleep and woken
my brother to drive me to the hospital, this man
who didn't even believe in using aspirin.

Every bump knocked my skull into the side
of the car. I focused all my effort
on the unresponsive muscles and managed
to move my head slightly away. After that,
I was able to sit up to breathe and see
where we were going.

At the emergency room, my brother reached
wild-eyed into the backseat to grab me. I pushed
his hands off, struggled to stand. "I'm in my underwear,"
I said; "I need pants and shoes." "You're coming,"
he said; "Either get to walking, or I'll carry you."

CL Bledsoe

I winced across the rocky lot, unsure with each step
if I'd move forward or fall or why
I was even there. It was the first visit
I could remember to a hospital. My father, who I'd never
seen ask for help with anything, ran ahead
to find a doctor, a nurse, anyone.

Duck Hunting

It isn't the waders, keeps you warm,
the shot of Kentucky Tavern bourbon back in the truck.
When you step in the water, sink
into that world between air and earth, reeds
slap you in the face like an old lover
and you forget to be cold, except you feel it, except you just don't care.
There's a job to do, and it's ducks.
                                    Your buddies fan out just enough
to feel that each man's alone, but if he moves you can feel the ripples
lap against you like wind, and you wait.

Someone makes the call and they come and it's so quiet
you could hear another man think, except no one is thinking; they watch.

Then the guns, the noise the ducks must think is God or it's the ground
falling up so loud it knocks the flight out of them, and the fall to water
is farther than they have flown in a season. If there are dogs,
you send them, wade deeper into the marsh
to collect the things you've taken from the sky,
then make your way back to land
                                where the cold reminds you
that you can die, and it's a long way home,
but you must never begrudge them their wings,
or you've sinned.

Ol' Man Ditch

Rains pump gumbo into rivers so thick
you can nearly walk across. There is a beating,
pushing them to the sea, but where is the heart
of Arkansas? Taste sweet rice on the slinking
breeze, Ol' Man Catfish hidden below the murk.
This is the wounded hart of Arkansas, lurking
under an old railroad bridge, waiting to feed
on old tires, the dead, a whole childhood's worth
of chicken livers. Ol' Man fries up soft but
you will never catch him, not with any old
store bought cane pole. The hairy chin of that longing
will wait and wait until your overalls don't fit no more.
Trade them in for slacks, then a suit, then the pine
pants that never shrink. Your children and their children
will dangle their poles into the water that's cold
(and deep, too) and yet he'll swim.

My Father Spreading Mayonnaise

My father spreading mayonnaise with a fork.
My father calling me sugar.
My father jumping off a tractor, lifting me from the hard clumps of dirt
where I fell, too scared to cuss me.
My father in the kitchen, reading as the sun comes up.
My father always carrying a rifle in his truck to shoot snakes as he cuts levees.
My father pushing my mother and then standing over her, scared.
My father taking his mother out of the hospital by force
so she could die at home.
My father asking how old I am.
My father catching me stealing from his wallet.
My father glaring at me and my shoulder-length hair at his sister's funeral.
My father falling out of his truck, drunk, and rolling down the hill.
My father lying on the couch for three days in DT.
My father telling me he loves me.
My father on the couch, uncomfortable in my apartment.
My father in his fuzzy house shoes, calling my fiancée sweetie.
My father drinking champagne in the rice field and listening
to big band music.
My father carrying his son-in-law through the house by the throat
after seeing bruises on my sister.
My father meeting his illegitimate daughter for the first time
in a soybean field and taking her fishing.
My father sending me hundred dollar bills through the mail.
My father walking through the woods quietly, with a gun but not hunting.
My father flirting with the girls at the grocery store.
My father's picture that looks like a young Ronald Reagan.
My father in uniform, on a ship to Japan.
My father at Nagasaki.

My father in a suit at his brother's funeral.
My father refusing to go to the hospital.
My father's red skin and black hair going gray, his legs, blue
and veined, his breath steaming in winter.
My father's smell of rain.
My father quoting Shakespeare while he skins fish.

Fence Building

Up on the ridge my father pulls barbed wire taut
between fence posts, and hammers staples into the wood,
his blows keeping time with his cussing.
"Couple months, they'll have worked these loose," he says.

On the ground beside him, the old rusted fence wire lies twirled
like a cobweb, some of the strands still twisted together
from when the boys squeezed through to hunt quail.

At supper we hear them popping birds out of the sky.
He scowls and concentrates on his mashed potatoes.
"Should we call the police?" Mom asks.
"They'll leave soon as they get a couple," my father says
and reaches across the table to spear another biscuit.

In the morning, we find the new wire twisted together
like frayed ends of thread, making a gap
where someone slid through.

My father untwists the wire. I catch him staring
over the fence at the hills, thin as bones rolling
under a dog's skin. "Ought to last the season,
anyway," he says.

Visiting Cousin Rob in Little Rock

His wife was blond and pretty like mom
used to be in pictures. Their house
was so clean I was afraid to sit, so I stood.

These people lived sober lives without fear
of the man screaming in the kitchen,
the woman dying in the bedroom, the smoldering
eruption of frustration, spiked down
like butterfly wings on a page for too long.

We left late instead of staying the night,
my brother grumbling, listening to Jethro Tull
on the radio. In the darkness of Fair Oaks, we came
to a railroad crossing. A train thundered past;

sudden clouds of fire engulfed the roof
of the locomotive. My brother turned
down a side road and paced the thing. The heat
wafted against us. The engine of his minivan
growled, angry as he pulled ahead. The highway
crossed the tracks, we turned and cleared the bump

airborne

for a moment, darkness all around except for that
fiery thing less than ten feet
away, bearing down on us.
I could see my brother's short hair
framed in fire.

Riceland

He slowed as it passed behind us, not even
blowing a whistle. The adrenaline
drained out of me, taking everything
else from that day with it, the fear,
the anger. "Why'd you do that?" I said.
"It's late," he said. "I didn't want to wait."
That wasn't it, but I knew what he meant.

CL Bledsoe

My Mother Making Donuts

My mother making donuts and jam in the kitchen piled with stacks
and stacks of dirty dishes.
My brother taking us on family drives in his Gremlin, Saturdays.
My father working half-days on Christmas.
My sister and I playing school until my mother started throwing dictionaries.
My mother eating bowlfuls of onions with ice cream and not leaving the
house for years.
My father taking me out to the fields to work with him.
My mother throwing tantrums.
My father staying out late, drinking while his buddies scold me
for trying to bring him home.
My sister sneaking out her window after my father threw her boyfriend out.
My brother reading westerns all day.
My father buying plastic sheets because my mother wet the bed.
My sister bathing my mother and trying to trim her fingernails
while my brother held her down.
Me feeding my mother tuna casserole.
Me at school, fat, in cheap clothes.
My father buying my mother a walker because she keeps falling down.
My father hiring a nurse to take care of my mother.
The nurse quitting.
My father hiring another nurse.
That nurse quitting.
My brother, my father and I dropping my mother off.
My father visiting my mother at the nursing home.
My mother not remembering.

Farmer's Tan

My father's arms lie; the red
of his perma-burned forearms stretches only
to the bottom of his shirt sleeves, from there
oaken muscles hardened by decades of rice farming,
covered by loose skin bleached the color of sun-faded paper
take up the fight. If you ignore that sagging face,
chin slumped beneath the weight of lies told
and heard, skip over the neck, a motley cliche,
and go straight to the chest, you'll see that same fragile skin
falling down to his black toenails, ruined by rice field water.

He offers me a stiff hug and I feel the halting muscles grip
and relax; stone slips into putty. Life will throw its booted foot
before his feet but few times, now.
This man, this stone pillar who could break me
as easily as glass in a child's hands,
has been worn down by water over the years.

Skin Cancer

Though they'd called his name, my father came back
to the waiting room and sat beside me, his hands still
and crowded in his lap, his fingers writhing like snakes,
two fingers for fangs.

"They're sharpening the knives," he said. I stared
at his face, the dark scab like caramel stuck
on his cheek. I expected to see him shake
like I would have, but he was quiet.

"What now?" I asked. He sat back, rigid
and still, a reed in windless waters.
"Wait," he said, showing thin lips
and curling his long fingers to strangle the air.

Stumbling

      Something in my soul's shin wonders
why I didn't run as fast as the wind   coming from the mouth of the
preacher
      he would soon be
          when my cousin drove up that day.

I'd no idea he'd come to make me cry
         smiled when I cried
            and said I was saved for it.
      I trusted him   kin that he was   but he was on God's time
         not mine.

      I thought it was talk
         that happened to turn hard   and personal
            my crosses   slowly dragged out onto the lawn
     for the neighbors to gossip about
so I talked   and he eyed me like an old tom
         waiting for a cracked door.

      And when the tears came   the sobbing good and steady
he asked me   if I accepted Jesus
         loved Jesus
            knew Jesus
     took him for a friend   I do   I said
         standing in the middle of the lawn
            sobbing like a hungry kitten.

And he smiled   shook my hand   packed
up his bible and drove away   leaving me to wipe my face
and go back to that place
that had been a home
and now would just have to make do.

House Keeping

Dad built the red-brick house with his own hands
which meant it was someone else's job
to keep it clean. Mom taught school until
she retired early, while a succession
of house keepers and nurses dumped bleach
in the toilet in the blackening bathroom, loaded
and unloaded the dishwasher, ducked the cobwebs.
Ms. Crossin lived with her forty-five year old
son, believed the Earth was flat, and the moon
landing was filmed in Arizona. She was older
than Dad, but that didn't stop her from putting
in her teeth to flirt.

She smelled of copper and sweat, deep-fried
hotdogs split down the middle and stuffed
with cheese for lunch, or sent me on my bike to buy
barbecue downtown. She threw out all of Mom's papers
she could find one day, said we were too old
to still be thinking about that, and climbed into my bed
if I lingered in the mornings. She asked questions
I couldn't answer or understand. Once, she wore nothing
but a raincoat to work. I hid in my bedroom until Dad
came home late that night. The morning after I was caught
stealing from the IGA store she found me sulking
in my room, backed me into a corner, and yelled,
"Do you think nobody loves you?" with greedy eyes
that hovered around my face like gnats.

Gumbo

Down the road, Linwood
had 40 acres of gumbo, waiting
to suck the sweat
from his body. He lost boots,
tools, almost a truck, once.
It pulled all the soul
from him and left him fat
and empty, nothing
holding him up but beer
and a grudge floating
like shrimp in soup.
He'd come by the Shack, grumble
and boast. "Wait'll that dries out,"
he'd say. "Best land in the county
if the price of beans would hold."
We didn't say anything,
only offered him a beer.

James Earl Ray

We didn't mind the day off
from school, but we refused solemnity, refused
to let them think they'd been proven right
by martyrdom   we were ashamed
      of nothing.

      We joked in the halls—
It's James Earl Ray Day, no school Monday!
And laughed when we saw the black kids
      stare.

      I'm thinking about this years
later in an ATM drive-through—a sign says Closed
For Lee King Day. Who's he? I wonder
before I realize they've buried
Dr. King's name behind Southern
      pride.

      I'm older, now, but that dumb and mean
kid I used to be still has his friends
to hide behind. I consider moving
my account, but the bank is closed until tomorrow.
      I have to wait
      and sit with this.

The Undertaker's Son

Through high school we dunked him in toilets,
trash cans when we could catch him.
Runt who never grew, as though
death couldn't find him
if he stayed forever small.

We sped by his house, ignoring
the circle of dirt worn into his yard
because his father, the one man in town who knew
how badly a life could end, was afraid
to let him venture any farther.

We passed without seeing
him ride around and around, in perfect arcs
always leading back to the beginning.

Tides

I have no memory of the womb   or the scant years
   of unadulterated greed until I grew tall enough
to see above my mother's knees   into eyes
   faded like ink stains washed from fabric
leaving only the memory of a mistake

and the idea that   the same way   it's not her fault   for dying
   that same way   it's not my fault   I stole
my sister's Madonna album
   threw it in the ditch and let mud and sewage bury it
Then   when she cried saying   Mom gave that to her
   it's not my fault   I couldn't save it   could only let it stay buried

Or that same way   I stole   baseball cards from Wal-Mart
   tucked them under my shirt   and snuck them out
every day after school   or toys   or magazines   or wallets

It wasn't me   Those ugly clothes   runny nose from hay fever
   so fat I'd stolen summer's supper   hoping to steal something I'd lost
These things wincing against the eye   in my head
   these are just images   They're not my fault
                              They're not my fault
                              They're not my fault
                              They're not my fault

When I was 15

Summer was hanging around our necks like a noose
when Karen and I decided to run away.
We sat on her bed, watching
her little brother watch us. She'd mouth,
"Save me," and I'd nod.

"Dad paid me ten bucks so you
don't fuck," her brother said every few seconds.
"Call him Dan, Dad lives across
town," she would say.

                              "If you want to make out,
I won't tell," he'd say and we'd kiss like fugitives.
Thirty seconds would pass, and he'd settle
his brown eyes on us like a vulture.
"Take me to the store to get some candy,
or I'll tell Dad you were fucking in here."

All we needed was a ride somewhere
they'd be too lazy to follow.
When her brother got off work, we went
over to his place and sat on his couch
while he talked about his tats. He had a chain
from his ears to his nose, his nose to his nipples,
and down to his dick. I stood
while she went to use the bathroom,
like I'd seen them do in old movies.
"You must really love her," her brother said,
and I sat back down to the quiet of her absence.

Riceland

After a couple hours we realized he
was a dead end. Her Dad lived next door, though.
He sat on the sofa, drank Jack Daniels and told me
about how making love to his new wife
was like fucking a jar of mayo.
"Don't get married, boy," he said. "Biggest
mistake you'll ever make," Then a drink.
When the bottle was empty, he left.

"There's a room back here," Karen said.
"The lights don't work but it's private." Then inside,
holding hands and no one could see. "You're
so sweet, I'll do anything to keep you," she said.
She told me about the scar on her arm where she'd stabbed
herself with an ice pick, about her step-father's ex-cop
hands, about how her mother had never seen him
naked because he weighed over five hundred
pounds, but she had, and I strained her blonde hair
through fingers I knew couldn't save her and listened.

CL Bledsoe

Pickett

Fever is taking my body like Sherman in Georgia,
burning a swath from my throat to my lungs as I lay here
trying to sleep, but there are children outside my window
and I can't even yell at them.

It's the cigarettes that did it, tobacco brought me down,
ruined my air so that even though I'm breathing out blood,
I still want more.

All I'm doing is waiting with my eyes on the last filter
I burned down, waiting for that one-more-last-one
to get me through the night. It'll be late then. I'll sneak outside
where no one will know that I'm owned,
and forget about the burnt sore I'll be coughing through
all the rest of the night, just to enjoy sucking on that fire.

I know this as surely as I know that I'm a fool
for ever being seventeen, standing behind the school
with the other rebels and passing around Marlboros
filched from our fathers. Back then,
it was all about holding it in without coughing
so we wouldn't look weak in front of our brethren.
Back then, it was all about mocking our fathers
with their yellowed fingers already digging our graves.

Roads

Winter, driving the gravel roads I almost
died on when I was 17 and stupid
enough to think fun was worth dying for,
and ice was a playground. That was
a lot of cars ago, worlds and years.

I knew a girl who made it the next year.
We were eighteen, seniors, and almost free.
It wasn't ice that got her, it was drink
and the night. The cops found her brain halved
from the windshield, the other girl in the passenger seat
screaming through bloody lips. But on one remembers
that one's name or the father of the unborn child that supposedly
lost its life that night.

I remember the dead girl's calves,
her breasts hopping beneath her shirt as she walked
the corridors of high school. I remember speaking
to her occasionally in the hall, and her speaking back.

I drove those roads for years. They snake from
the high school up Rabbit Road, then veer off,
lose their tar and wind around the airport
where the crop-dusters land,
then across the highway
to the cemetery south of town where
the Satanists are buried. Ghosts sprang from that one
like grass, because it wasn't hallowed ground,
or so kids said.

CL Bledsoe

                    We followed
those roads in every direction, pacing
out our home. They looped
back on each other, circled through
the wilderness so that we could drive
for hours and come out on a highway ten miles
from town. South, where my dad's family sharecropped
before I was born. Near the crossroads,
where kids went to sell their souls, or drink.

We could take them all the way to the Mississippi,
we could cover every inch of Arkansas,
the places no one remembered but the dead
and dying. Towns that weren't on any map
other than the ones in the memories of the young;
with names like Last Chance, Hard Times, names that said
something about what it was to live there.

We could take them as far as we'd ever heard of,
though that wasn't saying much. We could follow
them anywhere, but they were our home.

The Boys

tied rebel yells to their truck antennas
when they cruised the loop at Sonic.
They drove up slow and made sure
they weren't alone before turning in.
Couldn't be too safe from gangs,
they said. If they caught a black kid alone,
they'd drop off their girlfriends for safety
and follow him, force his car into the parking lot
of the old Jitney-Jungle, two, three trucks
full of grinning, yellow-toothed white boys
with bats, brass knuckles, wrenches. A couple
carried nooses for a joke. Mostly, they'd laugh
while the black kids beat feet.

In the school parking lot, they untied the flags
from their trucks so they wouldn't be suspended
and stalked the halls bragging about the tooth-necklaces
they were going to collect as soon as somebody
stood his ground. They talked about getting tattoos
but couldn't decide between crosses
or flags—they needed something to set them apart.
They'd never hide their dignity under hoods
like their daddies, never march
on city hall to be ridiculed. They smoked cigarettes
in the parking lot, picked fights
with the skinny freshmen, but dropped their eyes
when the older black kids strode by.

School

We are soft white meat thrown
into shark-infested waters. The boredom
of anti-intellectual totalitarianism,
the Prussian Model training us
for factory jobs that no longer
exist. Pretty girls are not to be
spoken to. Pretty boys have fists
and no conscience, but many,
many friends. Do not move
or speak or think or enjoy:
sit. And pay attention. There's going
to be a test.

There is only one speed
and it is idle. The greatest advancements
of humanity thud to the floor, raising
chalk dust in the still air and almost
waking us. Don't forget fear
instead of biology, fantasy
instead of science. Billions spent
on the stick of American Foreign Policy every
day, with carrot crumbs leftover to teach
our children to think
the right way.

Paddles

They carved notches in the handles,
or wrapped ragged tape around them

that was once white but faded to gray

from hand sweat. They wrote sayings
or gave them names like someone would

a ship or a pet. They painted them red

or painted racing stripes or flames down
the sides. The older the teacher, the more

elaborate the paddle, though coaches or any

male teachers often decorated theirs as well.
They'd hang them over the chalk board so all

the kids could see them, but this could imply

a lack of use. Some left them in a certain spot
on the desk for easy access. The youngest

and freshest might hide theirs in a desk, pale

and unadorned until the day they lost the class
and had to bring it out. The next day, it would

be painted, notched, hanging above the board.

CL Bledsoe

The City with a Smile

On highway 64 between Helena and Jonesboro,
a giant cross forced on the sprawl of hills dotted
with churches and fast food eateries; gas stations

and strip malls slowly succumb to vacancy
and horizon. Ranch-style houses splinter in all
directions. Trash and car washes. Train cars rust

in the shimmering heat, waiting for the freight
to come back, their tracks more wall than line.
Teenagers cruise from the bowling alley to Sonic

and back, park by Wal-Mart to neck or drive out
to Big Eddie Bridge to smoke pot and complain
while lightning bugs dance in the trees. There is

high school football and judging others. There is
Jonesboro, Memphis, Little Rock, if you can drive.
Summer fairs and satellite TV. Further out,

there are rice fields, a handful of dwindling factories
with their bags already packed for Korea. Wynne,
this sleepover town near enough but not Memphis,

founded on a spot where a train derailed. We thought
we were tough because we spent one dry-eyed year
in the run-down Junior High across the tracks

before moving to the new one in the middle of town.
We were wiser than Solomon in our packs,
more concerned with the price of each other's shoes

Riceland

than the usage, already learning to turn up our noses
at the secrecies of the heart. We were killing time until graduation
or sixteen and old enough to drop out without losing

our licenses. Vo-Tech meant half-days today, but Honors
meant a future. Teachers whispered to the few of us who'd listen:
study hard and you can go to college and never come back.

Remember

You wrapped the night around you like a shawl
and said that I never remember.
I watched your lips dance through the words
and didn't hear a thing.

The wind brushed thin strands of hay-colored hair
across your shoulders. You said something
about the way the lake captured the light
of the moon and held it. I watched your nipples
poke at the cloth of your shirt

as you said, "Love is like the moon and the lake,
two things forever separate
that sink into each other at night."
I nodded slowly

and tried to think of something clever,
but all that came to mind
was the time in the back of Stephen's car
when you asked me to spank you.

I put my arm around your shoulder
and considered my chances of getting oral.
Then you said, "She isn't even pretty, really."
"What do you mean," I started to say, but you cut me off.
"I could have you to myself, if I wanted."

"It's not like that," I said. "Let me explain."
But you leaned in close
and slipped something in my pocket with a
"Happy anniversary." I stood dumb
as you drew the moonlight into your eyes like a breath
and said that I never remember.

Alfred's Puppy

I told you that I missed you
        that I felt like a fool
        that I tried
        but you laughed
So I'll tell you about the time you laughed so hard
that you wet yourself at Alfred's party
        and were too drunk to notice
I'll tell you about how everyone else saw it when you bent over
        to pet Alfred's puppy
I smiled   and pulled you up into a hug
        But you pushed me away and bent over again
        so I let you

While I Lay Quietly

"You're so smart; well you don't know
what it's like to have them come at you," she said.
"Throwing your legs so wide they crack
like dead wood, so it leaves stretch marks in your skin,
that almost look like words."

I tried not to look at her face as she told me
that I couldn't know how nice they'd been
at first, with the small talk and the drugs
in the hotel room they'd rented to party.
And then them punching her between her legs
with fists like sledgehammers,
while her friend screamed in the bathroom.

I wondered how I would know
if every man I met was one of them,
if I should touch her shoulder.
I don't know what it's like
to have them come at me.
But as she stared through my dirty windshield
talking softly to the gray and brown gas station parking lot,
I felt as though I could see them
creep softly into the next room
while I lay quietly
asleep.

We Forgave

your eyes so dark their gravity pulled us close
when we meant to keep our full attention
on our wallets, your laugh that made us want
to watch the movies you stole all your clever lines from,
your style that made us glad you were putting our clothes
to good use by wearing them, because we knew
the next time we saw you, you'd be dead. This was what
it was to be sixteen, knowing we'd make eighteen
because we were too awkward to die. Drugs forgave all sins, turned
the eyes from acne and weight and lies. Weekends spent spray-painting
bridges were more than ritual. We were helping you sign your effigy.
Ahh, Jeff, we gave you all our lunch money, all the beer we stole
from our fathers, all the love women didn't want,
but you didn't die.

Grab Ass

I wonder if you're dead and buried in a short
coffin, beef-jerky muscles wasted on meth
and misanthropy, daddy's money long spent.

Was the aroma of Ben Gay and rot in the air
while all the ex-footballers cum used car
salesmen wept quietly in their hand-

kerchiefs thinking about the glory days? I wonder
if your cheerleader wife stayed when you lost
your hair. When you got inside her, was there

anything there? Did you even win your blond
medal? What a waste you were. Timmy,
you hated me because I saw through you

to the void where your soul should've been,
and I knew, no matter how fast you ran,
you'd never outpace it. But all I had to do was wait

to get past you. Timmy, I hated you because you ruled
the world from the inside, because you always won
even when you needed to learn how to lose.

Halcyon

We were always humping each other
on beds, against walls; one would mount

the other and thrust a few times before
trading punches and calling each other

faggot. We sat nervous through videos

our older brothers sold us, or stolen books
we took turns reading aloud from, each of us

fearing to stand, to go to the bathroom
and be labeled *masturbator*, not realizing

there's no other purpose for teenage hands.

We knew everything except how much
we didn't know. We swaggered so hard

we could barely walk, our sweat-smell
broadcast before us, hairy bodies on display

for no one but ourselves. We cared about

nothing, ate our full share of the world,
and sulked when no more was offered.

Portrait of My Mother as a House

The body is a house of many windows: there we all sit, showing
ourselves and crying on the passers-by to come and love us.
                                    —Robert Louis Stevenson

Say the clouds are miseries, drifting
          across the blue void of the sky's mind
          above me, older than they seem.

Say the winds are memories, pushing
          clouds, the fluff of despair that manages
          to come between the sun and the ground
          and therefore darken life.

Say the birds are wants, their wings flapping
          out wind, generating paths no one
          remembers they've built.

Say the power lines are needs, supporting
          the birds, but thinking the birds are keeping
          them up.

Say the ground is habit, holding
          the power lines up
          because it doesn't know anything else to do.

Say these windows are eyes, looking
          lest their light fade, darken
          and crack, so that all who pass
          are driven to misery, shed their flesh
          and jump into the sky to drift.

CL Bledsoe

Portrait of My Mother as a House II

Eaves leaning down like limbs straining under heavy snow;
I climbed on your shoulders, careful not to knock any shingles loose.

In the arms of the wind, I could see your heart bellow thumping
in time with the revolutions of the world.

I do not know you. You stand on top of the hill
up which I push my boulder. Littering the hillside

with pebbles. I'll name them, as you did me.
What more could I hope to do?

My Sister's Hair in 3 Decades

Late 70s

I have a picture—me, baby brother; inverted as a little blonde girl,
my sister who could swing a bat, climb a tree, punch
like any boy, holding me safe in her lap.
Her missing front tooth, hair
brown, down to her shoulders
because Mom wouldn't let her cut it shorter.
She spent years trying to pet dad's cows,
gave up and planted flowers in the yard
until the cows found them and nipped off their heads.

Late 80s

The name Menudo written on the carport
in shoe polish. The smell
of ozone dying in big sticky curls that will not move.
My sister, her Indian name: Little Mini-ha-ha (Dad's nickname),
her hair no longer tangled with brambles, turned black
as a raven's coat. Room full of noise
and friends I don't like. Boys
who haven't done as much as they'd like to think,
making jokes everyone understands, but no one wants
to. One of them went to prison for beating another boy
to death with a baseball bat. Another died
of a drug overdose. Me, interloper, curious,
lingering outside her door.
"Go away," she says. "I'm busy."

CL Bledsoe

Late 90s

The day I get my first apartment, my sister
comes over with bags of cleaning supplies, soap,
"Stuff you'll forget you need," she says, all
generic brands costing more
than she can afford, working poor with three kids.
Her hair straight, smart, deep black
with gray lines appearing like moonlight
reflected on water.

She hands me the bag and I'm
little again, playing the baker's man in her lap—
she dangles but doesn't drop me
on that old couch at Dad's house—
the one they threw out years ago.

Jonesboro

... Thanne longen folke to goon pilgramages
     —Chaucer, Introduction to *The Canterbury Tales*

1

Every year, a few days before Christmas,
we made the pilgrimage
to Jonesboro, nearest town with a mall.
Mom saved stamps all year
to trade in for plates, bowls; once,
she got a whole vacuum cleaner
while my father stood, shaking his head, saying
you don't get something for nothing.

We entered through Sears, admiring
the clothes we considered too pricy
any other time, then out to wander the Y
shaped corridors, my sister, stuck
watching me. There were cookies big
as steaks, tee-shirts with spray-painted
noise, the rush of people.

Christmas Eve, we stayed up
to stuff our stockings with the candy
and treats we'd saved up for all year,
hung them in the living room and lay in bed
till dawn, waiting to open the boxes, the contents
of which we'd already shaken, unwrapped, rewrapped,
and played with.

CL Bledsoe

2

On the way back from the mall, out of our heads
on youth and high school boredom, Quasi and I stole
a shopping cart, named it Bert and tried
to get pulled over. We wanted to be on Real
Stories of the Arkansas Highway Patrol. We drove
through all the small towns between there and Wynne
recklessly as we could (which was really just as bad
as everyone else). But, ever luck's fools, we made it home, kept
the cart (which we decided must be feeling very bemuzzled)
and waited for the next weekend, when we'd shed
our town like faded feathers and drive an hour back
to the mall, to stand, riffle, wait.

3

Joe L lived in a tower   facing another tower, in a room
with a bed and a closet.   Three of us crammed in, sleeping
on the floor, in chairs, feet propped on the sink, though
we had perfectly roomy   beds at home. He'd bring
day-old chicken patties in a greasy bag from the fast food
place at which he worked   and we'd fall on them like dogs.
This was college,   the closest some of us would get.
We took walks through   the Quad, smoking, long, laced
joints while Joe L told   stories of jumpers from the clock tower,
crazy men cussing the   students and calling it preaching.
One night, after several   days cooped up, Joe L no longer
even making the illusion   of attending classes, we went up
the stairwell, unscrewed   all the fluorescent lights, two of us
carried the bundle of   round glass up to the top floor
while a couple more   watched, below, taking pictures.
We pitched the tubes,   watched them   tumble, weightless,
and shatter perfectly   like water splattering on pavement,
and ran down to see   the pictures.

Just outside the door,   the dorm monitor saw Joe L, told
him to stop, the weight   of time suddenly settled back onto
our shoulders as we   snuck closer to hear, "Hey, you the
one selling that car?"   the man asked. "How much you want?"

4

I lived like a stray taken in by two
girls, both beautiful, both perfect
ly flawed in different ways, neither
interested in lugging the burdens of my
attentions on their backs. I never understood;
they were marking days till graduation, waiting
for their lives to begin. I took a gun away
from one before she could use it
on herself, talked the other through nights
of crying, gray mornings, and still went home lonely.
I was all desperation and good intentions, lost
and wild and fighting the pastels, the short-hairs,
the 401K. I never understood slacks;
I never understood tomorrow
instead of today.

The Bank

Dad said there was no future in the farm
he'd built with his brothers from the dirt
up, so he sent his sons off to bag

groceries, stock produce, flip
burgers while his brother and the bank
carved up the land and kept

the white meat. We knew fish
and cattle, rice fields and soybeans.
We knew jeans and family, sunup

to sundown, the names of the people
for whom we worked. My brother put in
thirteen years on the line before

being replaced by an elsewhere of lower
wages, looser laws. I cleaned a desk for nearly
a decade before standing in front of one

myself, giving my time to anyone who would
listen. Dad got old, took a position on
the couch, and filled his hours with TV

and crossword puzzles. These days he can't even
hear the trucks laying down a parking lot
in what used to be the family vineyard.

The Grocery Store

was just a mud puddle in the road
of life, my brother told me. I was starting
at the community college that summer, then
it was just a year until I could move.
A man can do anything for a year.

"I went to college," Johnnie told us
one morning. He was a third tier manager, short
and nervous like a dog that's used to being kicked.
"I dropped out," he said. "There wasn't anything for me there."
"What'd you study?" a kid asked.
"Piano," Johnnie said.
"I didn't know you played piano," I said,
suddenly surprised.
"I don't," he said. "That's why I went to college."

Work Clothes

I was raised by generations
of men whose idea
of dressing up meant putting
on a uniform, not
because they owned
just that, which was often the case,
but because they were proud.
The uniform states, simply: I can sit
in this restaurant
with my family, eating. I can have
a family, because I work.
I am part of this world.

Now, I sit, dressed better
in my banker finery than my father
at any funeral he's ever attended, watching
the men come in after (hard) work to cash
their checks, oil
stained, mud on their pants, stinking
of grease, sweat, their hands
dirty, calloused, complimenting
the girls (politely) who wait
till the men leave to laugh.

CL Bledsoe

Banker's Hours

"They leave food out, crumbs
all over the place," she
says. "And they wonder
why we have mice."

The drive-in is an assembly line, the hum
of production matched by Missy's
monologue. Old men cuss us
when we ask for IDs. When we ask for address verification,
old women threaten to close their accounts,
and drive away mid-sentence while we spiel.

Weeks out of college, I thought:
good benefits, holidays, at least it's not
boring. I tick each advantage off
on the list in my mind, not convincing anyone,
only preaching patience, the mantra of the beaten.

"My first week," she says, "they made me throw
a mouse away. They use glue traps,
and its fur was all matted and it squeaked. They laughed
at me for days when I cried.
That's when I knew, these people
have no souls."

Waiting

First it was earthquakes—the New Madrid fault
waking, spreading earth in a tired yawn.

They told us it'd be August; that hell month
when it's so hot even the mosquitoes stay in bed.

They wrote books prophesying our doom,
hardcover editions available for $24.95.

And we hunkered down to sweat and wait, hoping
at least our names would be saved

on some list up there. But the fault never woke,
and we had to go on, living, back to school.

Next it was meteors, coming to send us the way
of the dinosaurs. Reagan's Star Wars would save us,

but thanks to those bastard Democrats, we had no chance.
There would be a cloud of dust to block out the sun. Floods,

rains of fire, we might just as well be Pharaoh
begging Moses to lead his people out of here.

We almost welcomed that cloud
of dust, as it would've at least blocked out the UV rays,

which would give us cancer if we lived.
Then there was the greenhouse effect.

CL Bledsoe

This was aside from the day to day deaths, gang violence,
drugs, devil worshipers waiting in dark alleys

and Unitarian churches to snatch
our sinful souls. We didn't stand a chance,

what with Y2K and Jesus' return.
But He never came,

and here we all are still waiting, eating
our way through the days, hungry

for that final absolution
by anyone but ourselves.

Father

My father taught me to say I'm sorry
        regardless of guilt; it's the thing to do
        like taxes, work, traffic
these things fill the spaces in days.
And, if you study patience, or study man
        which leads to the same end
        you can achieve a sort of grace.
You can learn to enjoy the DMV, the 3 am feedings
        the snow;
        this is called thankfulness.
My father taught me this.

All of this flashes through my mind
        as I stand in his warm house
        on Christmas morning
and notice that his hand
so used to holding beer, bourbon, wine
        is reaching out for me.
But it's late and I have friends to see, family
        to surprise with my presence
        and gifts
        and all I can say is
        I'm sorry.

Relics

I have no memory of your voice. I can't rewind
and play it back like some tape recording in the spinning cogs

of my thoughts. I have no records, no paint
splattered on the walls of the cave

hollowed between our lives that we two grew within.

That cry I uttered when I was pulled from you,
splayed before the world is also forgotten.

So we are even.

The echoes have been long going,
but are now terminally forgotten, and I can mourn

the colors of all the days we missed by keeping eyes
solely on each other's throats, but they've passed.

Mother, outside, today, there was a purple fire
like Mars riding down to trample us all. The world burned,

and was renewed in light.
I just wanted to tell you.

Lonnie's Garden

Mornings when it was too wet to plant,
or afternoons when everyone else was drinking,
he tended the garden, producing perfect melons,
swollen, rich tomatoes,
strawberries that tasted like strawberries, squash
and eggplant and corn for the family, sweet stuff,
not even comparable to anything
from a store, same as his mother had planted for her house
since the Depression.

He planted two rows of greens over by the road
to keep the fish customers busy
so they wouldn't boss over the men's shoulders.
I remember those old women, dark
as unsweetened chocolate, stooping down to pick,
stiff from age and arthritis. The secrets they knew
of catfish and mustard greens,
one could only imagine.

I always marveled at his stamina. Summers,
after a day of rice farming. I was ready
to collapse, already slipping into the habit of laziness.
We watched TV sprawled out, ate, and did
nothing else. I didn't understand working hard in the waning sun
after a day already spent in toil, just for something extra,
tasty as it was. But he was already sweating when we pulled up
in the still rising morning.

The garden lay fallow for years after he stopped showing
his too much teased face around what was left of the farm.
a third of which was proven his
by law, and was slowly being sold off.
My brother took the patch over
to have something to complain about.
He gives my sister already rotting tomatoes, thin squash,
tasteless and sickly, and leaves it to the weeds for weeks at a time,
which is better than my own attempts at gardening.
Neither of us has the knack for it. Spoiled
by the saccharine sweetness of store bought veggies
for so long, we've forgotten the reward
of fresh, real food; we've made due for too long
sleeping in, seeing no need for inviting extra work.

Between Autumn and the Fall

My father has it all worked out.
    On Sundays in autumn
when everyone else is in church talking about the fall
    he's out gathering pecans from one of the trees
    he has scattered around the farm.

He takes them around to his sisters, wives of friends,
    all these old women he knows.
They all agree that he's a kind old man, considerate
    to a fault, and it makes them feel good
that he came by to visit and thought enough about them
    to bring them pecans.

Then they get to thinking he must be lonely
    without a wife to use those pecans herself
    and after a week or so they show up at his house
    with pecan pies, cookies, cakes.

    He's been doing this for years.
The women get to feel good about themselves, and my father
    confided in me that if he only knew a way
    to get them to make him ice cream
        he'd be set.

Hunting Rabbits

Last night   I dreamed   I trespassed   on my father's land
   poaching rabbits   with his gun   in the pasture   he used to own
Beyond the fence   I came upon a corpse   standing vacant

I crept through an open window   into what used to be our house

The floor   rotting and yellowed   like old paper left in an attic
   crumbled under my feet   The walls   slipped down
and I rammed the stock of the gun   under a corner and caught
   the ceiling   propped it up   on the kitchen table
which still had some life

There was a knock on the door   my uncle   that old dead man
   I barely recognized   held the carcass   of a rabbit
A red welt   stained its white fur

You been shooting your Daddy's gun, boy?   My uncle asked
   holding the rabbit   *No sir   but I'd sure love to have me
one for supper*   He handed over the body   and headed
   around the back   of the house

Didn't know you'd bought the place back   he said
   How's it coming along?   He kicked a piece
of rotted pine   *Slow going alone*   I said

He walked   a circle   around the house
   nodding and pointing   As I followed him   around
the last corner   he came   into the sun
   and faded   I could see   through him   down the hill

Riceland

to where my uncle's house   had been   I turned
  and my father's house   was gone   Dust   barely dented
the grass   where it once stood

I woke   in my own bed   the taste of game   in my mouth
  shoulder stiff   from the recoil   of my father's rifle
and for the rest of the day   nothing   could console me

The Wind

The pain in my head is simply the wind trying to
                                        spray
            itself out of my ears   my eyes   my mouth   but they are so full
                    of the blood of all the seasons before
and behind   (that it can't get out)   In the void of early
            evening   I can hear the creaking of trees stretching one last good one
                    before bed
the mad buzz of flies   tasting the dust
            thrown out over the day like a blanket
                    by the tiny fingers of plows   sifting the soil like change in a pocket

            I don't want to leave this place
                slow as time is here
            that part of me that feels the seasons change
as an itch in my skin   that can only be scratched
            by the nails of the sun   wants to stay the same here
            That part of me
                    that knows   the whys of growing things
that wisdom   trying to burst my skull
            and stay   knows there's truth here: man
                    was not meant to know
                            more than he can bear

Walking Through My Father's Fields, Home

The windows creaked from the heat
the day we bundled my mother up
and hauled her off like an old Christmas tree,
taking only a couple of suitcases
and her sickness with her—this dying stranger
who hadn't left the house
since before I could remember, and whom I'd sat watch over
for more than my 15 years—watched her wither
like a lake bed, until I was sure there was nothing left
of her but dust.

       Dad said,
"We're taking her to the hospital."
I pulled on pants good enough for town, and shoes,
as my father and brother led her out the door,
half the time carrying her and her confused moans
to the old International truck. I climbed in the back.

My father drove faster than usual,
which still wasn't very fast,
past the barn, the sheds and tractors, the fields.
My brother said the silage looked sparse,
and my father, that it'd gotten scorched by the drought
and we'd be lucky if it lasted the cows through winter.
I scanned the yellow blighted field as we rattled

down the long gravel road
peopled by cows that's jumped the fence
which we didn't stop for. They
grew small and quiet behind us

as the trees gave out, and the gravel
turned into asphalt with a bump.
The fields became houses.

The edge of our land bordered the county hospital.
We pulled into the cracked and ugly asphalt parking lot and waited
while Dad went to get an orderly.
Behind us stretched corn—I could barely make out the cows
grazing in the field—and beyond that the road, then the pasture,
and hills. Somewhere back there was the house,
just a mile or so away.

I turned back to the truck as they came for her.
My brother walked over to me
and pointed off to the south to the nursing home
they'd just built on a corner of layout ground
that used to be ours. That's where they'd take her
when she was all checked in, he meant.

We'd brought her into town so she could die proper.
If she made it through the year, she'd be able to see
our winter wheat outside her window and maybe think of home.
"Dad's finishing it all up," my brother said, "we can go."
I nodded and glanced at the truck.
Instead, we walked to the barbed wire fence,
which was overgrown with a wall of trees and weeds.
We scaled it and plodded through the still young corn,
not speaking, growing slowly separate
as we spread out to drive the cows
back to pasture.

About the Author

CL Bledsoe is the author of 5 novels including the young adult novel *Sunlight*, the novels *Last Stand in Zombietown* and *Necro Files: $7.50/hr + Curses*; 4 poetry collections: *Riceland*, _____*(Want/Need)*, *Anthem*, and *Leap Year*; and a short story collection called *Naming the Animals*. He's been nominated for the Pushcart Prize 8  times, had 2 stories selected as Notable Stories by *Story South*'s Million Writers Award, had 2 others nominated, and been nominated for Best of the Net twice. He's also had a flash story selected for the long list of *Wigleaf*'s 50 Best Flash Stories award. He blogs at Murder Your Darlings (clbledsoe.blogspot.com). Bledsoe reviews regularly for *Rain Taxi, Coal Hill Review, Prick of the Spindle, Monkey Bicycle, Book Slut, The Hollins Critic, The Arkansas Review, American Book Review, The Pedestal Magazine*, and elsewhere. Originally from Arkansas, Bledsoe lives with his wife and daughter in Maryland, where he works as a teacher and college counselor.

Publication Credits

Poems in this manuscript originally appeared in the following journals in similar forms:

Alba, Apalachee Review, Arkansas Literary Forum, Arkansas Review, Aurora Review, Barnwood, Big Muddy: A Journal of the Mississippi River Valley, Blue Collar Review, Blue Ridge Literary Prose, Bolts of Silk, Canopic Jar, Caper Literary Journal, Clackamas Literary Review, Concho River Review, The Dead Mule, Exposure, Free Verse, Flint Hills Review, Grasslimb, Kaleidoscope, Lifelines, A Little Poetry, Margie, Maverick, Nerve Cowboy, Nimrod, Orange Room, Poesia, Poetry Southeast, Red Booth Review, Southern Hum, Sow's Ear Review, Spillway Review, Stickman Review, Story South, Thunder Sandwich, Thrush, Toasted Cheese, Verse Wisconsin, Westview, Wisconsin Review.

"Envoi," "Huntington's Disease: Brushy Lake, Thanksgiving, Avon, Johnny Hill, Bus Stop, The Hill," "Chairs," "But My Legs Remember That Road," "My Father Spreading Mayonnaise," "My Mother Making Donuts," "Visiting Cousin Rob in Little Rock," "The Bank," "Relics," and "Walking Through My Father's Fields, Home," appeared online as a chapbook entitled *My Mother Making Donuts*, available at *The Dead Mule.*

"The Old Ways" also appeared in the Bottom Dog Press Anthology *Family Matters: Poems of Our Families.*

"The Bank" was nominated for Best of the Net, 2010.

"Roaches" was selected as the winner of the Blue Collar Review's Working People's Poetry Contest for 2004.

Praise for *Riceland*

In *Riceland*, Bledsoe is unswerving in his depiction of the
beauty, despair, and bludgeoning cruelty of life on an
Arkansas farm. Be prepared—stark and startlingly revealing,
these poems will sear your soul.

—Jo McDougall
Author of *Dirt, Satisfied With Havoc,* and *Daddy's Mystery*

CL Bledsoe's *Riceland* is full of natural wonder. Bledsoe pays
attention and documents daily life with skill and cunning and
we are lucky to have such a poet in our midst. At times he
reminds me of Jim Harrison, in his ruthless eye for man's
connection to nature and his search for balance in an
increasingly severe world. Bledsoe writes equally well about
farming, about the physical world, about place, and about
family. Riceland is a book to contemplate, to help see through
a true poet's eyes and to read again for its hard-won grace
and gentle wisdom.

—Corey Mesler
Author of *Some Identity Problems* and
The Ballad of the Two Tom Mores

"I know how to grow things, and I know how to kill them,"
writes CL Bledsoe in *Riceland*, a book set in the rice fields and
dirt roads of rural Arkansas at the end of the 20th century.
Bledsoe captures the darkness, violence, and longing of a
young man growing up at a time when so many family farms,
like his father's are going under. The death of the family farm
is the larger theme, but the poems about his mother—and his

inability as a child to understand the Huntington's disease that cripples and eventually destroys her—are the heartbreaking heart of the book. In a world that makes no sense, he approaches adulthood "wishing time would stop, speed up, something." Although he tells us, after a dream of rabbit hunting on the lost farm, that "nothing could console me," there is a consolation in the dark beauty of these poems.

—Ed Madden
Author of *Signals* and *Prodigal Variations*

In *Riceland*, CL Bledsoe has written about his childhood in rural Arkansas, which is something I'm an expert on, having lived one myself. Growing up in places like that is all about animals, alive and killed; big, rough fathers you love and fear; mothers and sisters you can't understand. Bledsoe captures it all beautifully in this skillfully written arc of poems, filled with images of memories of a childhood which, like most childhoods, is fully tied to place. This place is *Riceland*.

—Dale Wisely
General editor, RightHandPointing.com and
LeftHandWaving.com

Few books have the kind of thematic integrity one finds in *Riceland*. *Riceland* reminds me of how I felt toward Sherwood Anderson's book, *Winesburg, Ohio*. Bledsoe presents the experience of what it was like to grow up in the redneck south in the Mississippi River Delta in one of the poorest areas of the country. This is what Bledsoe does so well, he tells us unforgettably what it was like to live there—there in Eastern Arkansas where a father raised soybeans, rice, cattle, and catfish to make a hard-earned living. Bledsoe offers scraps of life with many lines that will be remembered. The fact that Bledsoe grew up out of this experience to become the writer he has become only makes the story and the struggle more remarkable. *Riceland* is a singular book by an exceptional poet.

—Peter Krok
Editor of *Schuylkill Valley Journal*
Author of *Looking for an Eye*

Other Titles Published by unbound CONTENT

82154670R00077

Made in the USA
Lexington, KY
26 February 2018